HAL•LEONARD®
BASS PLAY-ALONG

AUDIO ACCESS INCLUDED

QUEEN

PLAYBACK+
Speed • Pitch • Balance • Loop

To access audio visit:
www.halleonard.com/mylibrary

3350-2011-7961-6425

Cover photo: Getty Images/Mark and Colleen Hayward / Contributor

ISBN 978-1-4584-0495-4

Visit Hal Leonard Online at
www.halleonard.com

Contact Us:
Hal Leonard
7777 West Bluemound Road
Milwaukee, WI 53213
Email: info@halleonard.com

In Europe contact:
Hal Leonard Europe Limited
42 Wigmore Street
Marylebone, London, W1U 2RN
Email: info@halleonardeurope.com

In Australia contact:
Hal Leonard Australia Pty. Ltd.
4 Lentara Court
Cheltenham, Victoria, 3192 Australia
Email: info@halleonard.com.au

Another One Bites the Dust

Words and Music by John Deacon

Ah, _____ take it! Bite the dust! _ Bite the dust, _

_ ah! Hey! An -

Bridge
N.C.

oth - er one bites the dust. _ An - oth - er one bites the dust. _ Ow! _ An -

oth - er one bites the dust. _ Hey, hey! _ An - oth - er one bites the dust. _ Hey. _____

(Em)   (Am)

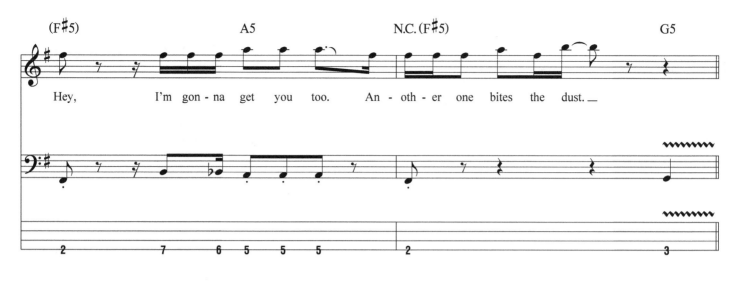

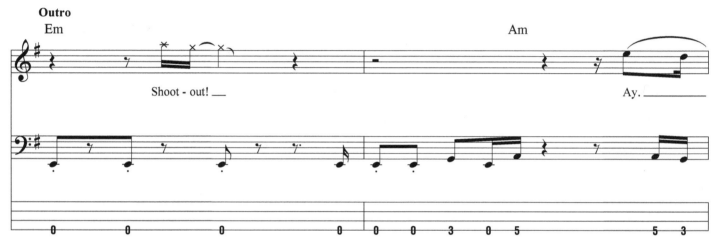

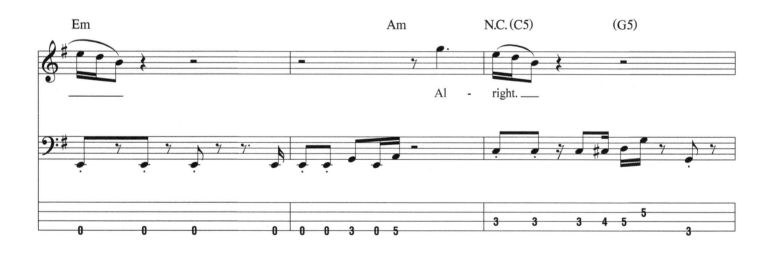

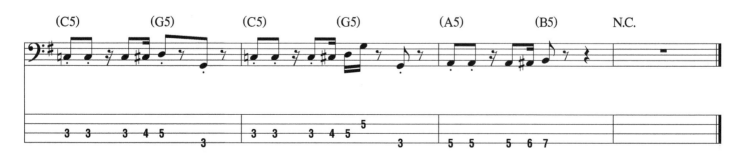

Fat Bottomed Girls

Words and Music by Brian May

Drop D tuning:
(low to high) D-A-D-G

Intro
Moderately ♩ = 86

Bass tacet

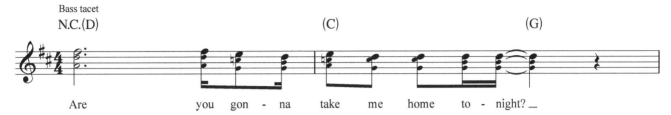

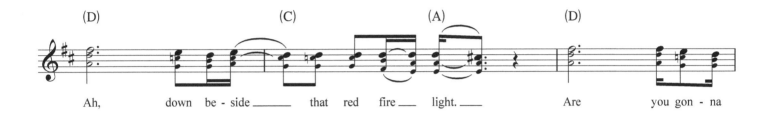

Are you gon - na take me home to - night?

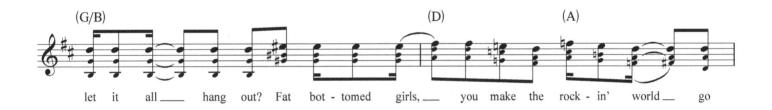

Ah, down be - side that red fire light. Are you gon - na

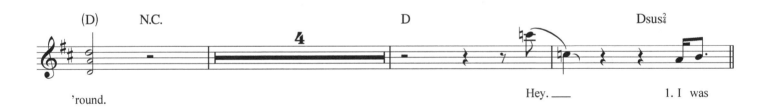

let it all hang out? Fat bot - tomed girls, you make the rock - in' world go

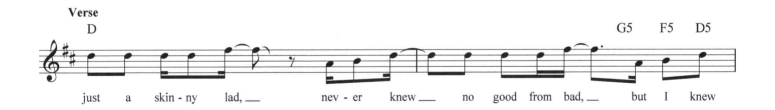

'round. Hey. 1. I was

Verse

just a skin - ny lad, nev - er knew no good from bad, but I knew life be - fore I left my nur - ser - y. Huh. Left a - lone

with big fat Fan - ny, she was such a naugh - ty nan - ny, heap big

wom - an you made a bad boy out of me. ___

Hey, hey. _   Woo! _

___

Verse

2. I've been sing - in' with my band 'cross the wa - ter, 'cross the land, _ I seen

mf

let ring

ev - 'ry blue - eyed floo - zy on the way. _____ Hey.   But their

Them fat bot-tomed girls, they get me. Yeah, yeah,

(Fat bot-tomed girls. ___

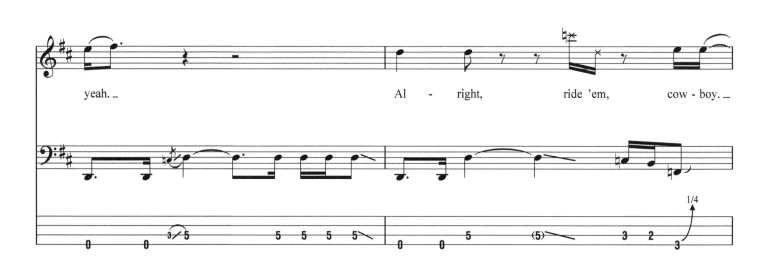

yeah. _ Al - right, ride 'em, cow - boy. _

Woo!

Fat bot - tomed girls.) ___

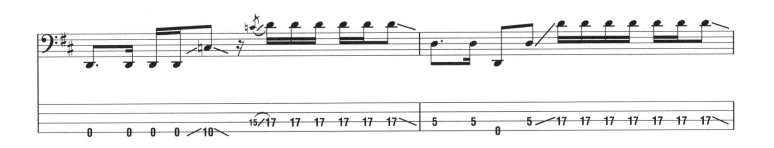

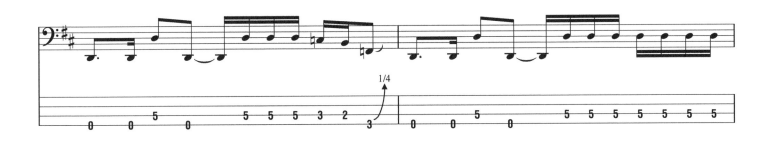

Crazy Little Thing Called Love

Words and Music by Freddie Mercury

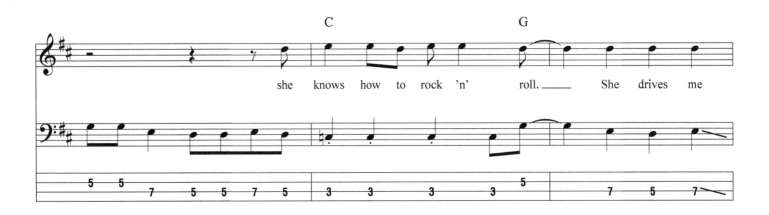

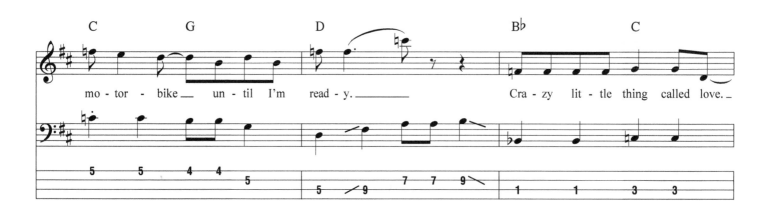

mo - tor - bike ___ un - til I'm read - y. ___ Cra - zy lit - tle thing called love. ___

Guitar Solo

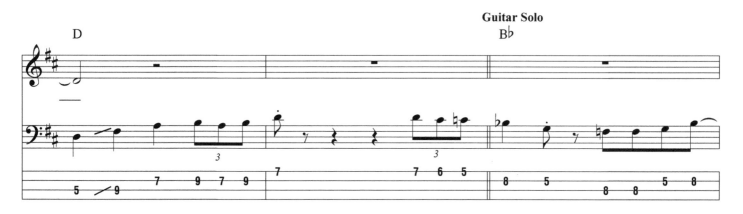

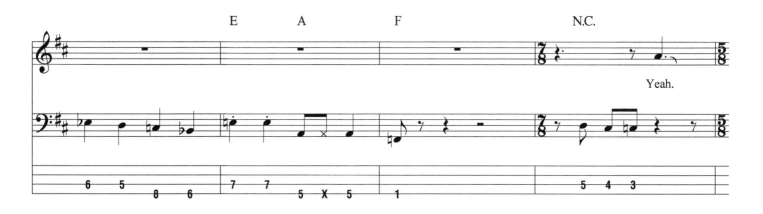

Yeah.

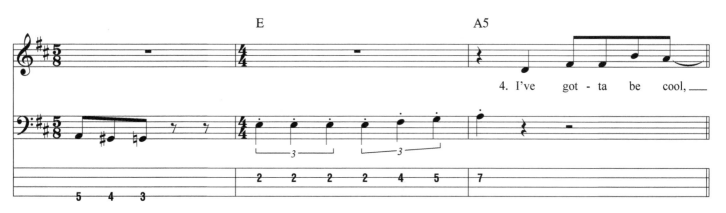

4. I've got - ta be cool, ___

Verse

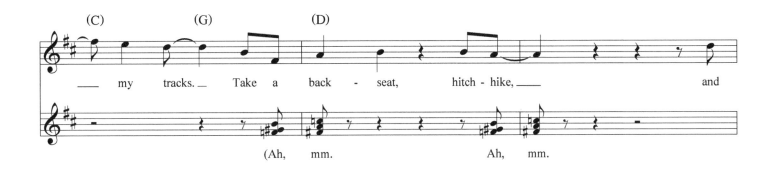

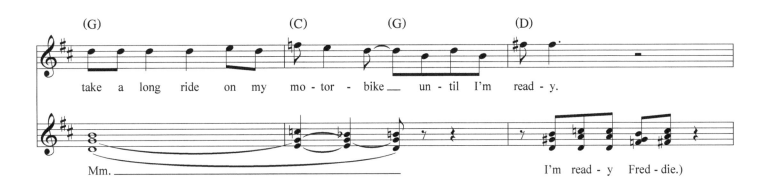

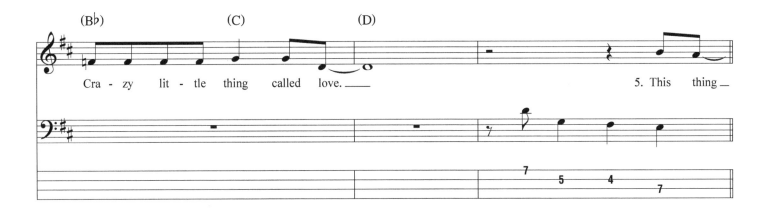

Verse

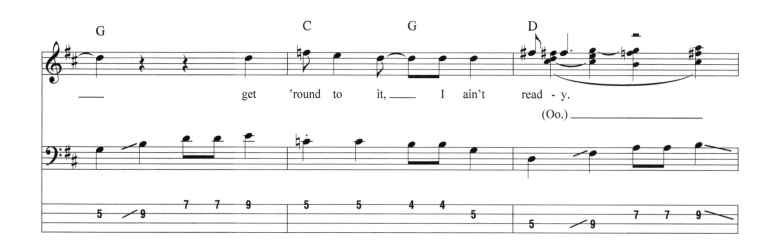

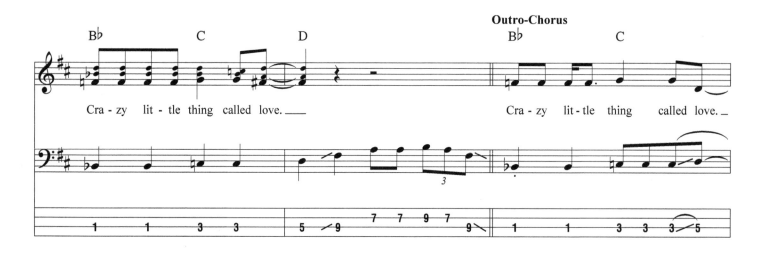

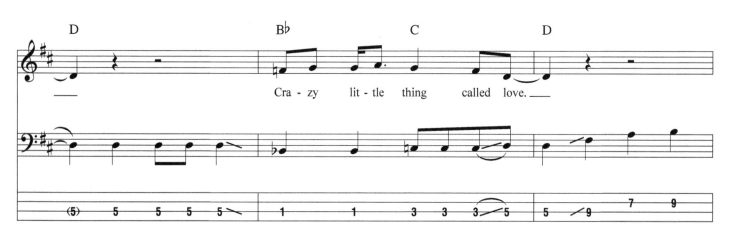

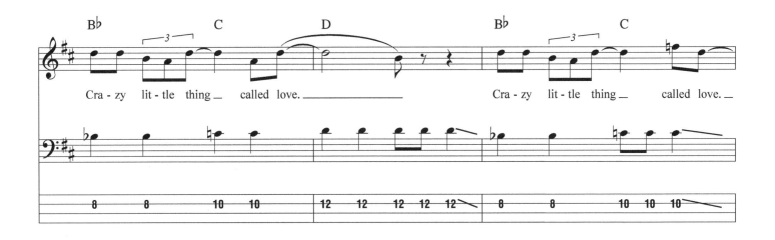

Cra - zy lit - tle thing __ called love. _____ Cra - zy lit - tle thing __ called love. __

Begin fade

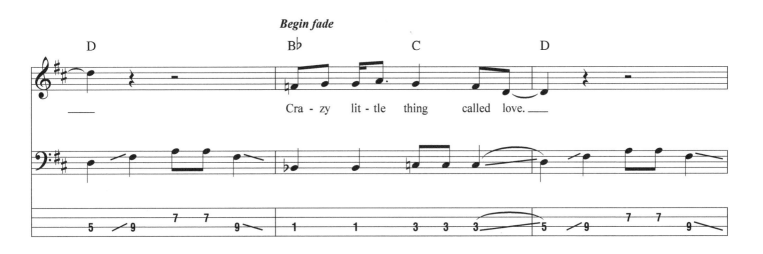

__ Cra - zy lit - tle thing called love. __

Cra - zy lit - tle thing called love. Cra - zy lit - tle thing called

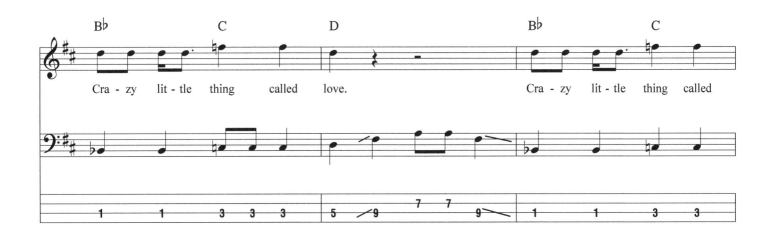

Fade out

love. Cra - zy lit - tle thing called love. __

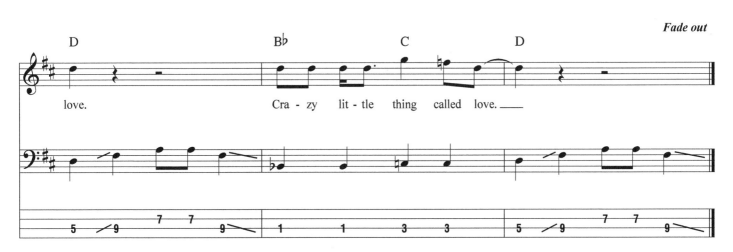

Killer Queen

Words and Music by Freddie Mercury

A Kind of Magic

Words and Music by Roger Taylor

No mor - tal __ man   can win this __ day. __

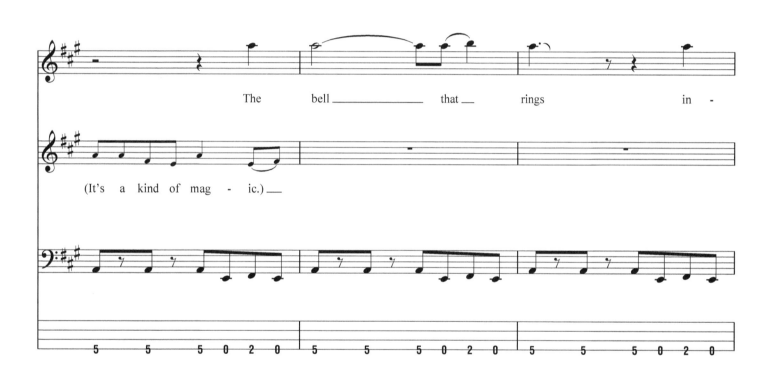

The   bell _____ that __ rings   in -

(It's a kind of mag - ic.) __

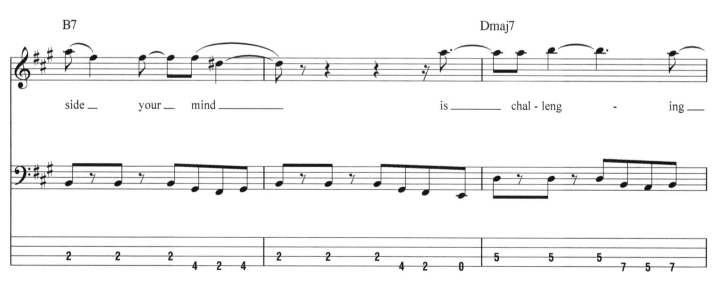

side __   your __ mind _____   is _____ chal - leng   -   ing __

35

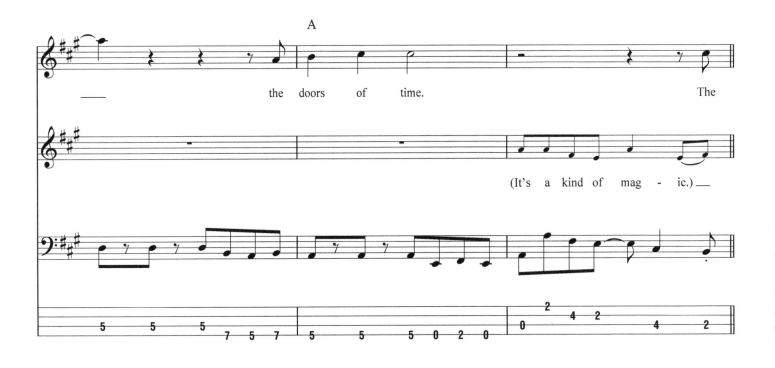

A

the doors of time. The

(It's a kind of mag - ic.)

Pre-Chorus

F#m7　　　　　　　　　　　D

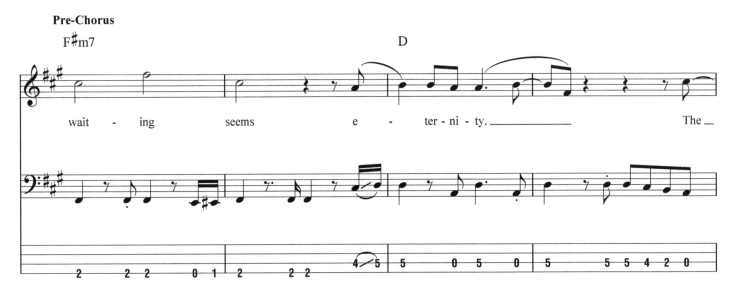

wait - ing seems e - ter - ni - ty. The

F#m7　　　　　　　　　　　E

day　will dawn　of san - i - ty. Is

(Ah,　oo.)

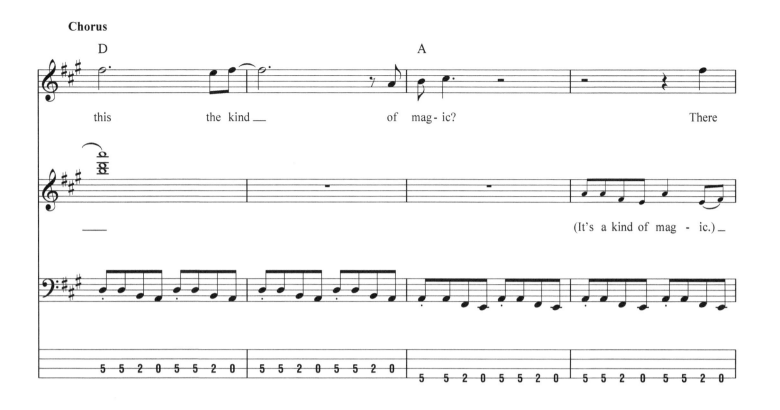

this the kind of mag - ic? There

(It's a kind of mag - ic.)

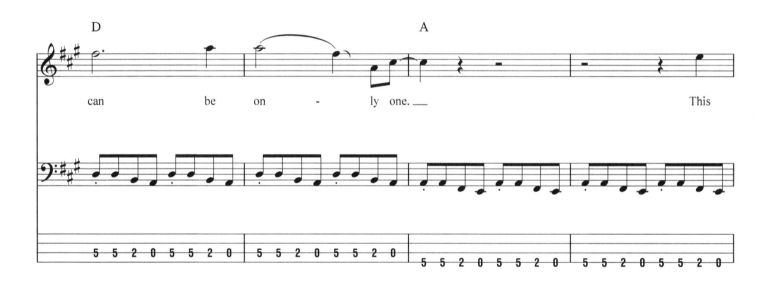

can be on - ly one. This

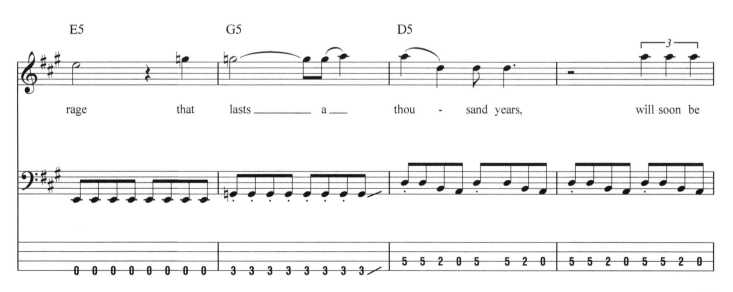

rage that lasts a thou - sand years, will soon be

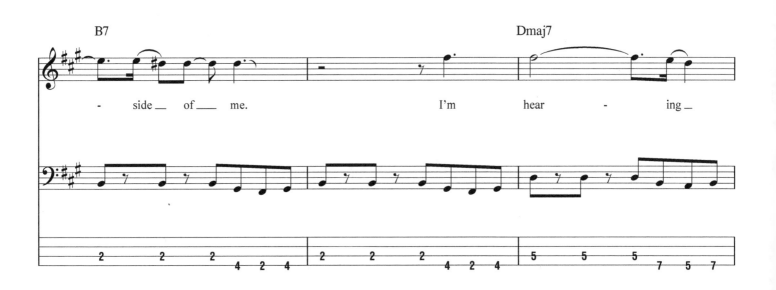

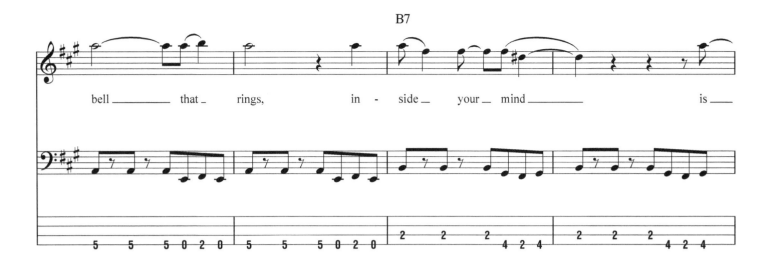

bell _____ that _ rings, in - side _ your _ mind _____ is _

_____ chal - leng - ing ____ the doors of time. _____

Interlude

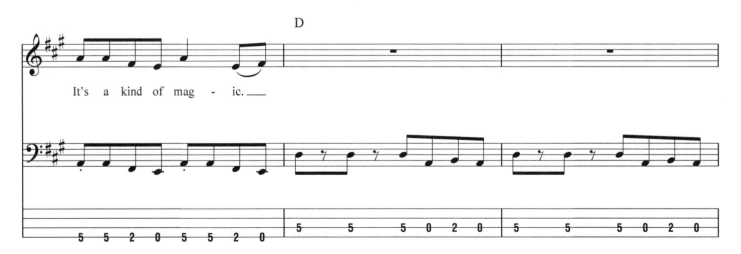

It's a kind of mag - ic. ____

It's a kind of mag - ic.

5 5 2 0 5 5 2 0   5 5 0 2 5 5 0 2   5   5   5 5 0 2 0

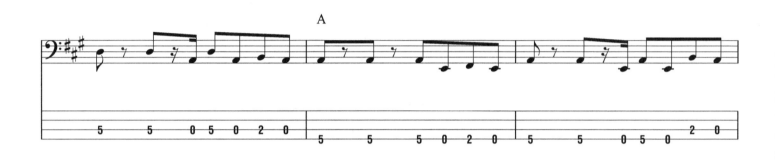

5   5   0 5 0 2 0   5   5   5 0 2 0   5   5   0 5 0   2 0

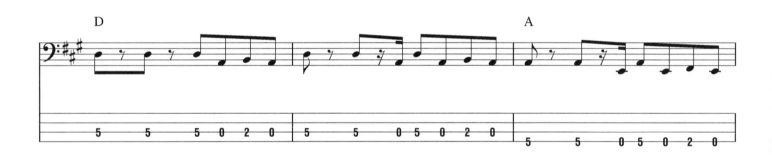

5   5   5 0 2 0   5   5   0 5 0 2 0   5   5   0 5 0 2 0

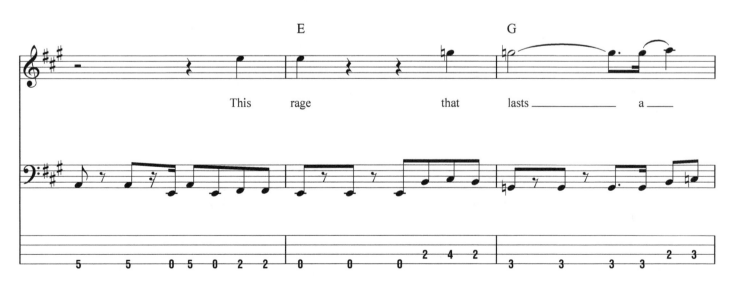

This   rage   that   lasts _____ a ____

5   5   0 5 0 2 2   0   0   0   2 4 2   3   3   3   3 2 3

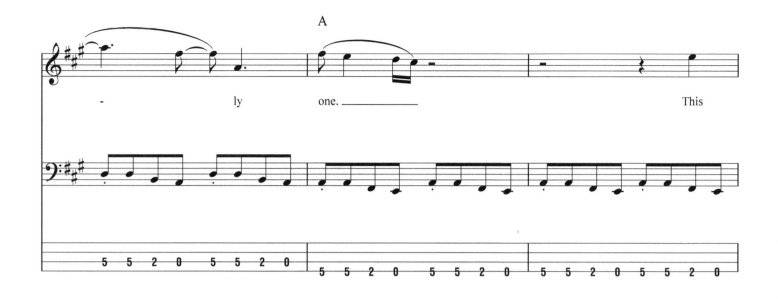

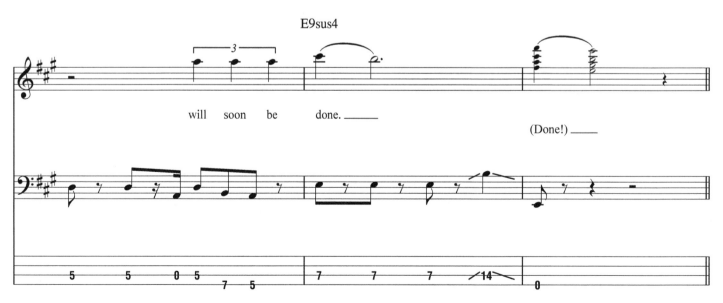

Outro

Stone Cold Crazy

Words and Music by Freddie Mercury, Brian May, Roger Taylor and John Deacon

3. Walk-ing down the street shoot-ing peo - ple that I meet with my

rub - ber Tom - my wa - ter gun. _____ Here ___ come the dep - u - ty, he's

gon - na come and get ___ me, I got - ta get me get up and run. _____ They got the

si - rens loose, I ran right out _____ of juice. ___

___ They're gon - na put me in a cell. If I can't go to heav - en, will they

Outro-Chorus

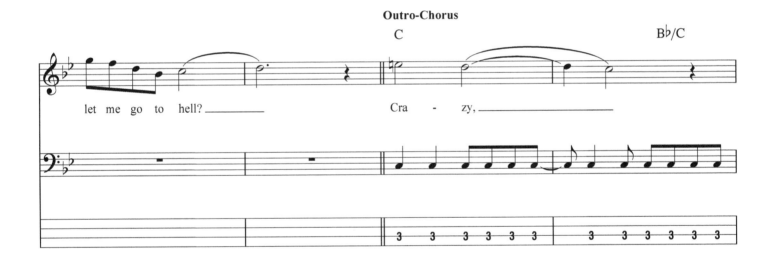

let me go to hell? _____ Cra - zy, _____

stone ___ cold cra - zy, ___ you know. Ow!

Tie Your Mother Down

Words and Music by Brian May

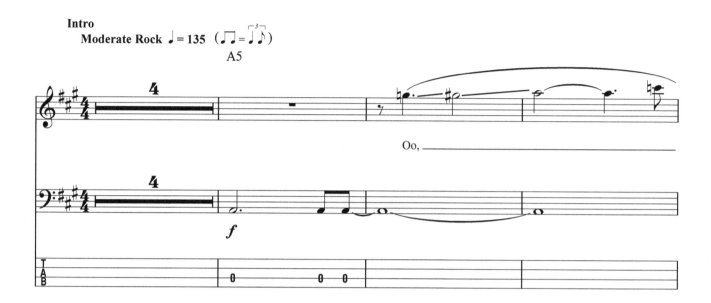

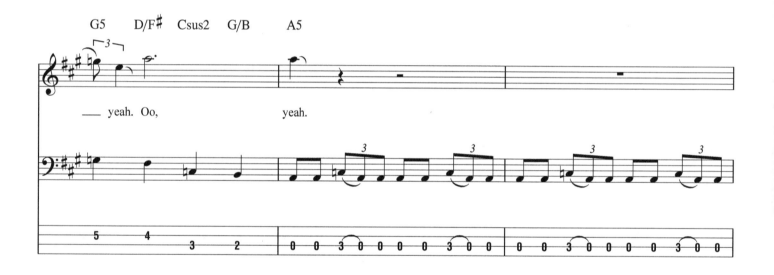

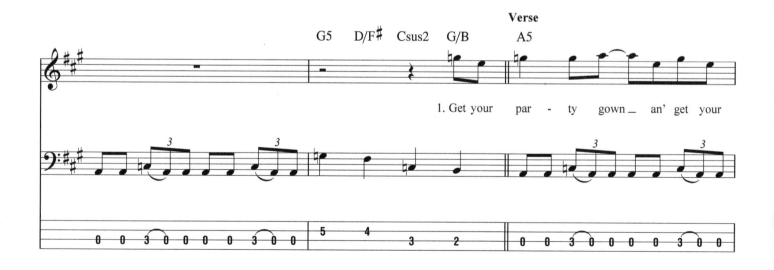

Oo. __ Tie __

Chorus

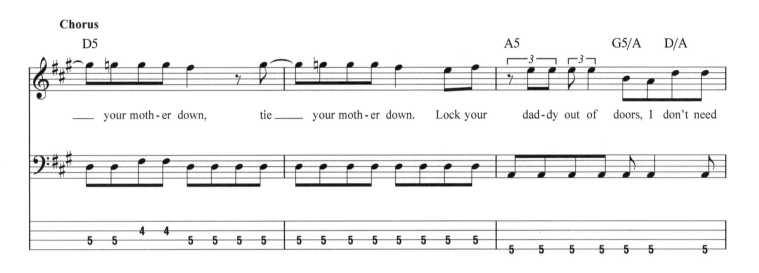

__ your moth-er down, tie __ your moth-er down. Lock your dad-dy out of doors, I don't need

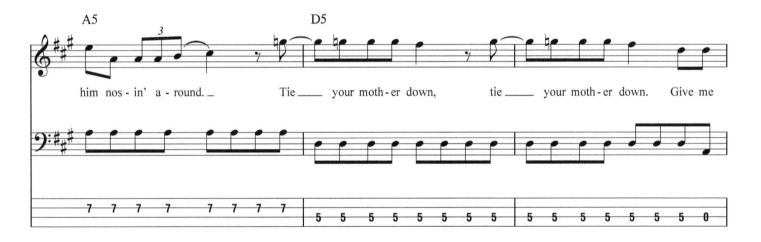

him nos-in' a - round. __ Tie __ your moth-er down, tie __ your moth-er down. Give me

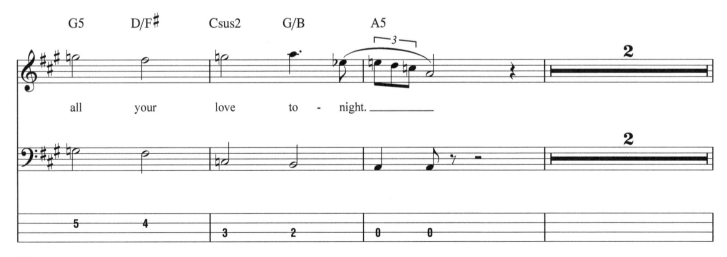

all your love to - night. __

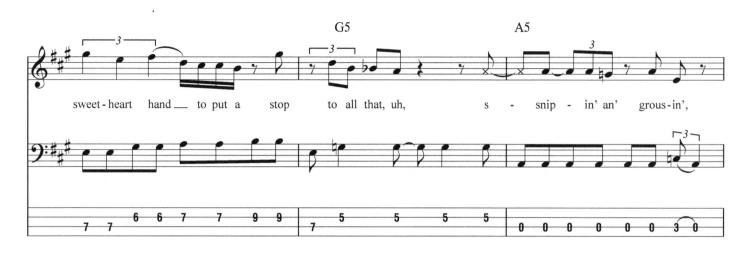

sweet - heart hand ___ to put a stop to all that, uh, s - snip - in' an' grous-in',

Chorus

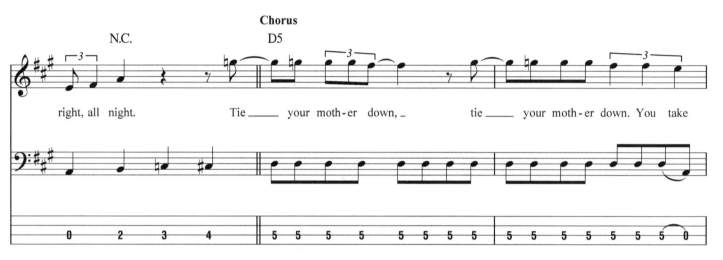

right, all night. Tie _____ your moth-er down, _ tie _____ your moth-er down. You take

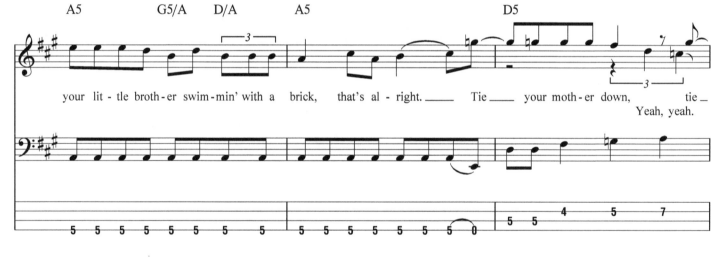

your lit - tle broth - er swim - min' with a brick, that's al - right. _____ Tie _____ your moth-er down, tie _

Yeah, yeah.

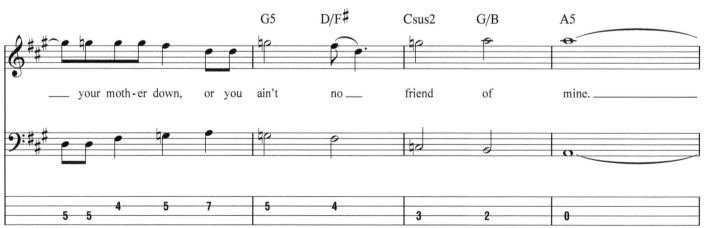

_____ your moth-er down, or you ain't no ___ friend of mine. _____

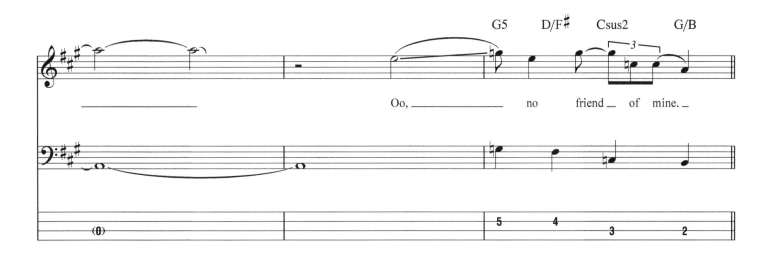

Oo, _____ no friend _ of mine. _

Guitar Solo

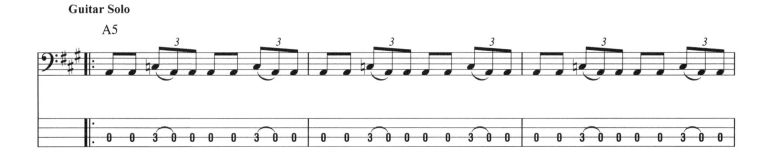

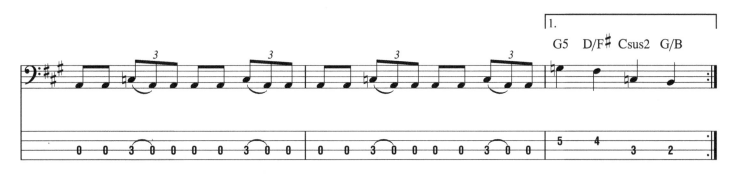

We Are the Champions

Words and Music by Freddie Mercury

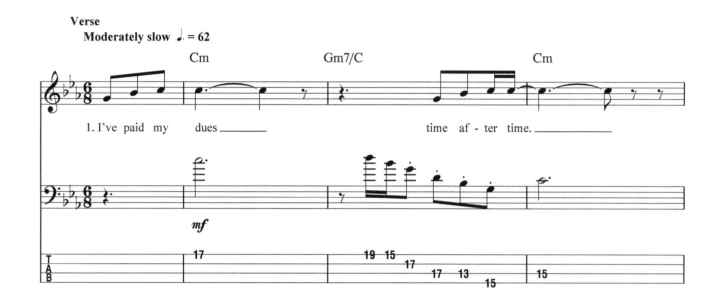

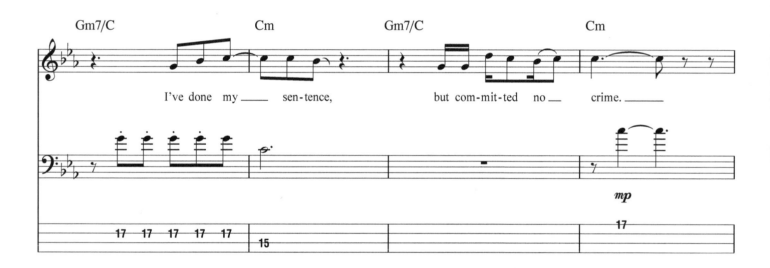

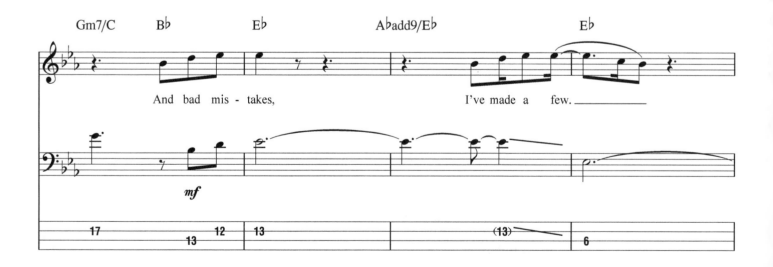